BASKETBALL

Alison Hawes

Editorial Consultants

Adria Klein

Cliff Moon

Lorraine Petersen

Frances Ridley

HAMERAY
PUBLISHING GROUP

Published in the United States of America
by the Hameray Publishing Group, Inc.

Every effort has been made to trace copyright holders
and obtain their permission for use of copyright material.
The publisher will gladly receive information enabling them
to rectify any error or omission in subsequent editions. All
facts are correct at time of going to press.

Text © Rising Stars UK Ltd.

Published 2008

Author: Alison Hawes
Editorial Consultants: Adria Klein, Cliff Moon,
Lorraine Petersen, and Frances Ridley

Cover design: Button plc
Cover image: Alamy
Text design and typesetting: Andy Wilson
Publisher: Gill Budgell
Project management and editorial: Lesley Densham
Editing: Clare Robertson
Technical adviser: Alan Sweetman-Hicks
Illustrations: Patrick Boyer: pages 24–25, 32–33, 38–41
Oxford Illustrators and Designers: pages 8, 12
Photos: Alamy: pages 4–5, 9, 10, 11, 13, 20, 29,
Corbis: pages 4, 5, 12, 14, 15, 35, 42, 43
Empics: pages 6, 18, 19, 21, 22, 23, 26–27, 34, 36, 37
Getty Images: pages 8, 9, 11, 16, 17, 18, 19, 30, 31
Andre Nichols: page 28

ISBN 978-1-60559-003-5

Printed in China.

1 2 3 4 5 PP 12 11 10 09 08

This book should not be used as a guide to the sports shown
in it. The publisher accepts no responsibility for any harm
which might result from taking part in these sports.

Contents

Basketball

Basketball is a team sport.

It is fast and action-packed.

Basketball fact!

Basketball was invented in 1891 by a gym teacher named James Naismith. He used a football and peach baskets!

It is played by men, women, girls and boys.

If you want to play for a team you will need to be fit and practice those moves!

Basketball Gear

You don't need a lot of gear to play basketball.

A light, loose shirt keeps you cool and lets you move easily.

Light, loose shorts keep you cool and let you move easily.

Soft, thick socks stop your feet from getting blisters.

Air-cushioned sneakers stop your feet from getting sore.

Play safe!

✗ No zippers

✗ No buttons

✗ No watches

✗ No jewelry

✗ No loose laces

Basketball Court

Basketball is played on a court.

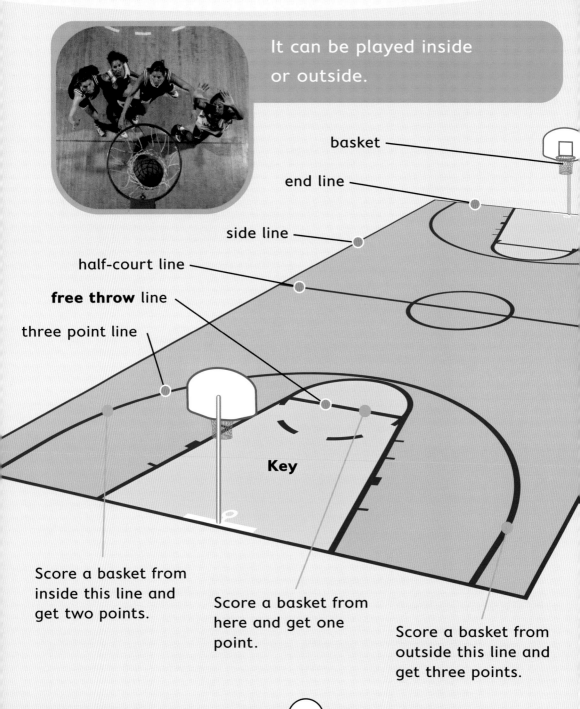

It can be played inside or outside.

basket

end line

side line

half-court line

free throw line

three point line

Key

Score a basket from inside this line and get two points.

Score a basket from here and get one point.

Score a basket from outside this line and get three points.

The basket is made up of a hoop and a net.

The hoop is 10 feet from the ground.

The basket has a backboard which is made of wood or plastic.

backboard

hoop

net

The ball

A basketball is made from rubber or leather.

It is full of air. But it still weighs up to 22 ounces! (That's as heavy as a pair of your shoes.)

Basketball Teams

School

Some schools have a basketball team. This is a good place to learn all the basic moves.

You can play against teams from other schools.

Recreation center

Some recreation centers run a basketball club after school. This is another good place to learn the moves and play for a team.

Look on the Internet to find your local recreation center.

No Team?

In the park

A park is a good place to practice the basic moves.

Some parks have a basketball court. Others just have a hoop and backboard.

At home

Invite some friends over and practice those shots!

The Team

A basketball team has up to 12 players.

Just five players are on court at a time.
They play in different positions on the court.

Team positions

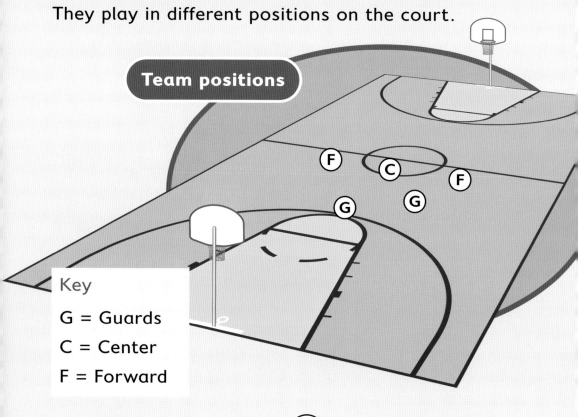

Key

G = Guards
C = Center
F = Forward

The guards tend to be smaller, quicker players.

They are good at dribbling and passing.

Guard

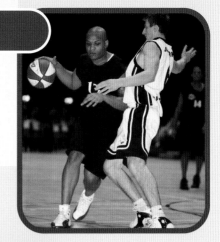

Forward

The forwards tend to be taller players.

They are good at shooting, passing and getting the **rebounds**.

Center

The centers tend to be the tallest players.

They are good at jumping, shooting and getting the rebounds.

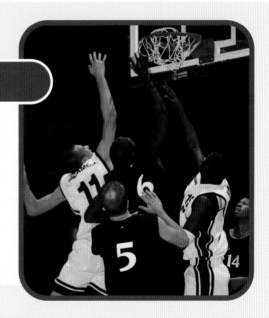

But a basketball team plays all over the court.
Everyone needs to be good at all the basic moves.

The Moves

Passing

In a fast game like basketball, you must keep the ball moving.

So get passing!

The chest pass

Use two hands.

Hold the ball at chest height.

Push the ball to your teammate.

Use a chest pass when there is no defender in the way.

The overhead pass

Use two hands.

Hold the ball at head height.

Push the ball to your teammate.

Use an overhead pass when there is a defender close to you.

Use one or two hands.

Hold the ball at hip height.

Bounce the ball to your teammate.

Use a bounce pass when you need to get around a defender or under a defender's arms.

Dribbling

Use one hand to bounce the ball.

Keep the ball close to you as you run.

Only dribble when you can't pass!

Passing is quicker than dribbling.

15

Shooting

Basketball is won by scoring points.

You score points by getting the ball into the basket.

So get shooting!

The lay up shot

Use this shot when there is no defender in your way.

The set shot

Use this shot for a free throw if you are close to the net.

The jump shot

Use this shot if there is a defender very close to you.

Defending

When the other team has the ball,
you must stop them from scoring.

So get defending!

When to defend	How to defend
When the other player is shooting	◎ Use your arms and jump to stop the ball
When the other player is passing	◎ Bend or jump to stop the ball ◎ Use your arms
When the other player is dribbling	◎ Bend down and get in close ◎ Use your arms
When the other player misses a shot	◎ Keep your eyes open ◎ Get ready to catch the ball when it rebounds

Basketball Shots

All the top players are good at the basic moves.
But they are good at trick shots like these too.

Slam dunk

A slam dunk is
a trick shot.

Players jump above
the basket and stuff
the ball in the net.

Reverse jam

The reverse jam is
an even harder shot.

Players do a slam dunk
with their back to
the basket.

Hook shot

A lot of the top players use this shot to score a basket when a defender is very close to them.

Trick dribbling

Some players can dribble the ball behind their back or between their legs!

Basketball fact!

In 2003, an American basketball player dribbled a basketball 108 miles in 24 hours!

Against the Clock!

Basketball is fast because it is played against the clock.

So move fast! Think fast!

If you run out of time, the ball goes to the other team.

The eight-second rule

When your team has the ball, they have just eight seconds to get it over the half-court line.

The 24-second rule

When your team has the ball, they have just 24 seconds to shoot at the basket.

The five-second rule

When you get the ball, you have just five seconds to start to pass, shoot or dribble it.

The three-second rule

When your team has the ball, no one on your team can be in the other team's key for more than three seconds.

Time out

Your team can call **time out** five times in a game.

Each time out lasts one minute.

Teams use a time out to talk **strategy**!

Wheelchair Basketball

Wheelchair basketball is a fast, action packed sport.

Many players use a special sports wheelchair.

A sports wheelchair is light and easy to move around in.

Basketball fact!

Wheelchair basketball was invented to help soldiers wounded in World War II to get better.

Basketball fact!

Wheelchair basketball was first played in the **Paralympics Games** in 1960.

Wheelchair basketball is now played in over 80 countries.

Canada beat Australia to win the gold in the 2004 Paralympics.

A Bad Move (Part One)

Josh's dad had a new job. It was miles from their house, so they had to move.

Josh's mom and dad wanted to move. Even Josh's kid sister, Liz, wanted to move.

But Josh didn't. He hated the idea.

Josh said, "If we move, I'll miss my friends. And I won't get to play basketball for the Tigers again!"

But like it or not, Josh had to move.

At the new house, Dad put up Josh's old basketball hoop.

"There you are," said Dad. "That should make you feel a bit more at home!"

But Josh just walked away.

He knew his dad was trying to help. But it was no good.

He just didn't want to be there.

Continued on page 32

Going to a Game

Going to a top basketball game
is fun – and noisy!

There is clapping and stamping.

There is chanting and cheering, hooting and loud music ...

... and there's a fast, action packed game to watch!

Basketball People

Lots of people help out at a basketball game.

Timekeepers

There are two timekeepers on the court.

One stops and starts the game clock and times the time outs.

The other stops and starts the 24-second clock.

Scorer

The scorer counts the score, the fouls and the time outs.

The coach trains the team and decides on team strategy.

The coach decides when the **subs** go in and when time out is called.

Referees

The referees control the game.

They make sure the players stick to the rules.

Referees' Signals

The referees use a whistle and hand signals to control the game.

See if you can spot any of these signals if you watch a game.

Some common hand signals

two free throws

one free throw

time out

Hand signals for fouls

traveling

holding

charging

pushing

A Bad Move (Part Two)

The next day, Josh was in a better mood.

He went into the driveway to practice his basketball shots.

He remembered what the Tigers' coach had told him and took a shot.

There was a clonk.

The ball hit the backboard and dropped into the net.

The boy next door heard the clonk and looked over the fence.

He watched, as five shots out of five dropped into the net!

"You're good," he called. "But not as good as Michael Jordan. He could make a shot with his eyes shut!"

Josh grinned and shut his eyes.

There was a clonk as the ball hit a window.

Josh opened his eyes.

There was a crack in the window!

Josh grabbed his basketball.

"Quick, let's get out of here!" he said.

Continued on page 38

Michael Jordan

Michael Jordan is an American basketball player. He is one of the most famous basketball players in the world.

People say Jordan can shoot baskets with his eyes shut!

Basketball facts!

Michael Jordan wears size 13 basketball shoes.

Air Jordan sneakers are named after him.

Michael Jordan Fact File

Born	**February 17, 1963, New York**
Height	**6 feet, 6 inches**
Weight	**216 pounds**
Basketball position	**Shooting guard**
Average points scored in a game	**30.1**
Teams he played for	**University of North Carolina** **Chicago Bulls** **Washington Wizards**
Retired	**2003**

Did you know?

Michael was in a movie with Bugs Bunny.

The movie was called Space Jam.

The Harlem Globetrotters

The Harlem Globetrotters are an American basketball team.

They're the most famous basketball team in the world.

The Globetrotters are famous for their basketball shows.

The shows are full of trick shots and stunts.

The Harlem Globetrotters have helped make basketball popular outside of America.

They began playing basketball around the world in the 1950s and a team still tours the world today.

Basketball facts!

A Harlem Globetrotter holds the world record for a 12-foot vertical slam dunk.

The tallest player to play for the Harlem Globetrotters was "Dut" Mayer. He is 7 feet, 6 inches tall!

A Bad Move
(Part Three)

The two boys ran down the road.

"I'm Max," said the boy from next door.
"We'll go to the park, Zack is playing there."

Josh and Max watched Zack and his friends.
They were all good players.

Josh asked if he and Max could join in.

Zack looked at Josh and Max and laughed.

"Sorry, dude. You two are too small to play basketball."

"But that's not fair!" said Josh. "You don't have to be a giant to play basketball!"

But it was no use.

Zack just walked away.

"Come back when you've grown some!" he laughed.

Continued on the next page

Later that week, Josh and Max went to the fair.

Josh's dad said they had to take Liz too. He was still angry about the broken window.

Zack and his friends were there.

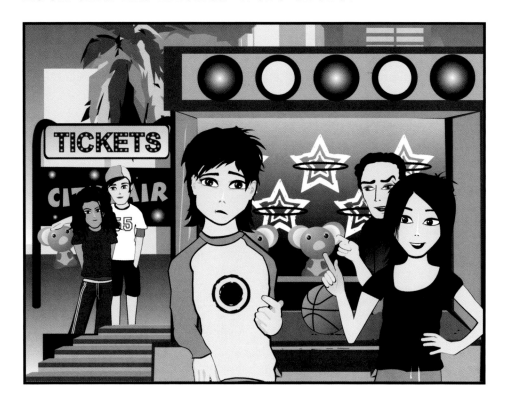

Liz saw Zack win a prize at the basketball game.

"Win me a prize!" Liz said to Josh.

"Yes! Win your girlfriend a prize!" laughed Zack.

Josh felt like hitting him.

Josh breathed deeply and took a shot.

There was a clonk as the ball hit
the backboard and dropped into the net.

Josh shot five baskets out of five.

Zack and his friends had stopped laughing.

Zack went up to Josh.

"I was wrong about you, dude," he said.

"We play for a team
at the recreation
center. Why don't
you come along
next week?"

"I'll think about it,"
Josh said.

Josh, Max and Liz
walked away.

"I think I'm going
to like it here!"
Josh grinned.

Olympic Games

Basketball became an Olympic sport for men in 1936.

The American team won the first gold medal for basketball.

The man who invented basketball was at the 1936 Olympic Games.

He gave the American team their gold medals.

Basketball fact!

At the 1936 Olympics, basketball was played outside on sand!

The Americans played their best team ever in the 1992 Olympics.

This team was so good it was called the Dream Team!

They easily won all their eight games and the gold medal.

Michael Jordan was on the Dream Team.

Quiz

1. What kind of sport is basketball?

2. Who invented basketball?

3. How high from the ground is a basketball hoop?

4. What do forwards need to be good at?

5. Which is quicker, passing or dribbling?

6. What is a slam dunk?

7. Why does a coach call time out?

8. Why was wheelchair basketball first invented?

9. What is the referees' signal for pushing?

10. What size sneakers does Michael Jordan wear?

Glossary of Terms

free throw A free shot at a basket. A free throw can be given by the referee when he/she sees a foul. Free throws are taken from the free throw line on the court.

key The restricted area on a basketball court. (See the shaded area on the diagram of a court on page 8.)

Paralympic Games The Olympics for people with disabilities

rebound A ball that hits the rim of the basket or the backboard and bounces back into the court when a shot at the basket is missed

strategy How teams plan to use their skills to beat their opponents

subs This is short for "substitutes." The substitutes are the players that sit on the sidelines until they are chosen to swap places with a player on the court.

time out When the game is stopped. Teams can take five time outs in a game to discuss strategy. This is called "charged time out". The referee can also call time out when a player is injured.

More Resources

Books

Basketball
DK Eyewitness Books
DK Publishing (ISBN-10:075661063X; ISBN-13:978-0756610630)
Includes color photos, history and superstars of basketball.

Basketball in Action, Sports in Action
John Crossingham
Crabtree Publishing Company
(ISBN-10:0778701743; ISBN-13:978-0778701743)
Explains rules of the game and shows the basics of shooting, passing, and dribbling.

The Kids' World Almanac of Basketball
Bill Gutman
World Almanac (ISBN-10:0886877768; ISBN-13:978-0886877767)
Fascinating basketball facts, from the history of the game to the NBA'S newest teams.

Magazines

Slam (Primedia, Inc.)
This is an American basketball magazine. It is full of NBA news, interviews with NBA players and lots of great photos.

Sports Illustrated for Kids

A kid's version of the popular sports magazine includes football, baseball, and other sports. Also has a great website at *www.sikids.com*

Websites

www.NBA.com
If you are into basketball this is the site for photos and news of all the NBA stars.

www.bballone.com
Player profiles, news, and statistics.

DVDs

Space Jam
Warner
A fun family movie, mixing cartoon characters and real life basketball players like Michael Jordan.

Coach Carter
Paramount
This movie is based on the true story of Ken Carter, a basketball coach of a struggling school team. Good story and plenty of basketball action.

Answers

1. A team game

2. James Naismith

3. 10 feet

4. They need to be good at shooting, passing and getting rebounds.

5. Passing is quicker than dribbling.

6. When the player scores a basket by jumping above the basket and stuffing the ball down into the net

7. To talk team strategy or because a player is injured

8. To help injured World War II soldiers get better

9. Both arms out in front; hands facing forwards in a pushing motion

10. Size 13

Index